The Beginner's Guide to Seed Saving

Learn Expert Techniques to Best Harvest, Store, Germinate, and Keep Seeds Fresh For Years in Your Own Seed Bank

TJ Books

Contents

Introduction

Discover the timeless practice of seed-saving—an ancient art that has stood the test of time for thousands of years. From preserving the genetic purity of historical plants to embracing self-sufficiency, seed-saving has captivated the hearts of both seasoned gardeners and beginners alike.

In the vast sea of seed-saving information, confusion often takes root. Many books assume a certain level of gardening knowledge, leaving readers frustrated when their saved seeds fail to sprout or succumb to diseases. But fear not! Our book is here to demystify the process, providing you with clear, step-by-step instructions and troubleshooting tips.

Whether you have some experience gardening or you're a complete beginner, we've got you covered. Our comprehensive approach ensures your success in growing your favorite plants, harvesting their seeds, and preserving them for future seasons. We leave no stone unturned, offering guidance from start to finish.

Our book embraces the unpredictable nature of gardening, acknowledging that not everything goes according to plan. When setbacks arise, you'll be equipped with the knowledge to troubleshoot and find solutions to keep moving forward. We believe in empowering you to navigate the ups and downs of the gardening journey.

Saving seeds goes beyond a mere hobby—it's a deeply satisfying endeavor. As you witness the fruits of your labor sprout from tiny seeds, a sense of pride and self-sufficiency will blossom within you. Imagine the joy of providing your own homegrown bounty to your loved ones, while also enjoying substantial savings on seed purchases. It's an incredible journey toward independence and nourishment.

Unlike other books that only scratch the surface, we go the extra mile. Our comprehensive guide covers every aspect of seed-saving, ensuring you have a thorough understanding of the process. From seed collection to storage techniques, we provide you with practical and actionable information, so you can confidently embark on your seed-saving adventure.

With this book, you'll discover the expert secrets to effective seed-saving. You'll gain an incredible and important skill that you can pass down to your descendants. You'll save money, and increase your health by having access to freshly picked produce that is packed with nutrients. With each successful harvest, you'll gain a deeper appreciation for the miracle of life and the intricate connections between plants and people.

Are you ready to take the plunge into the world of seed-saving? Let us be your trusted companion as you acquire the skills and knowledge to harvest, store, and grow your own seeds. Get ready to sow the seeds of self-sufficiency and reap the bountiful rewards of this fulfilling journey.

Let's dive in!

Chapter 1

Book I: Introduction to Seed Saving

<u>The Importance of Seed Saving in Gardening</u>

Seed saving is such an important part of preserving genetic diversity and ensuring the future of humanity's food supply. Pandemics, natural disasters, war, and disease will always threaten the crops the world relies on for nourish-

ment. To protect against these risks, governments and organizations have created giant seed banks to secure a wide
variety of plants for our future generations.

But individual gardeners can also play an important role
in maintaining biodiversity, by practicing seed saving themselves. Seed saving involves collecting seeds from the
produce you have grown, food you have purchased from the
store, seedlings or seed packets, for use in your own garden
and/or for exchanging with other gardeners. This not only
ensures that you will have access to a wide variety of vegetables, herbs and fruit, but it also helps to maintain genetic
diversity, which is essential for future success in growing
crops.

In order to successfully save seeds, it is important that you
understand what kind of seeds are best suited for saving.
You see, not all seeds are created equally. While some seeds
can keep well over time, others cannot.

By taking up seed saving as a hobby or practice, you can
become part of a larger movement that's working towards
preserving genetic diversity and protecting our future food
supply against any potential threats. As well, you can rest
easy knowing that you and your loved ones will always have

ample food to live off of, no matter what is going on with the food supply on a larger scale.

Benefits of Creating a Personal Seed Bank:

Rising Food Prices

Food prices have risen in the initial three years of the Covid Pandemic, living costs have escalated by 65%, and increased by an additional 12% since the war between Russia and Ukraine began. With the worldwide cost of living crisis putting pressure on household spending, many people are looking for ways to save money. Food prices are literally rising faster than the rate of inflation, so it's no surprise that people are trying to cut down their spending at grocery stores.

More and more people have wisely turned to growing their own fruit and vegetables. Most beginners buy seeds, which can cost several dollars per packet, and those who choose to purchase seedlings will find themselves spending even more. While cultivating your own garden will undoubtedly save you money in the long run, you can go one step further by growing food from your own saved seeds absolutely free!

Quality and Taste

Gardeners are not in control of the seed business. A seed variety that produces the most amazing fruits or vegetables, that have the perfect texture, and delicious flavor, and is just the right size, might be discontinued. Or worse, the seed company may run out and never replace its stock. Or, the seeds may change due to a change in soil conditions, climate, too much demand resulting in over-farming, etc. This can make high-quality seeds that produce great-tasting produce difficult to find.

If you harvest and preserve your own seeds, however, you will always have access to the high-quality seeds that produce the fruit and vegetables you enjoy so much. In fact, by creating a seed bank, you can store those seeds away for future years to come.

Self-sufficiency

The feeling of autonomy and accomplishment you get from growing your own produce is unlike any other. From gathering, preserving and sowing the seeds, to tending, nurturing and harvesting them - you can do it all yourself!

Preppers understand how essential it is to be self-reliant - especially in these unpredictable times. Now, while we don't believe in being doomers, and we don't advise you to be either, we recognize the importance of being ready for anything. It's much better to stockpile food than to risk not being ready when disaster strikes and having to scramble along with millions of people.

Having a stockpile of seeds means you can put aside any fear of running out of supplies. There's nothing more reassuring than that.

Healthier Food

When you use your own seeds to grow food, you will know exactly what has been done to your produce. You don't need to worry about whether your seeds have been genetically modified or exposed to "organic" pesticides, or diseases. Many seeds bought commercially are contaminated with pesticides and harmful chemicals. In fact, many seeds are purposefully treated with pesticides and antifungals to "protect" seedlings and preserve them. These chemicals can be harmful to insects, birds and small mammals, and are partly to blame for the worrying decline in bee populations. The same pesticides that are proving catastrophic for animals can also pose a threat to you and your family. In fact, some experts have directly linked all sorts of chronic illness-es directly to pesticides, herbicides and other chemicals.

"It's okay, I'll just buy organic food," you might be saying. Well, sure, but even then you must do your research to ensure that you are not still consuming harmful chemicals. This is because food production companies are still allowed to label their produce as "organic" even if they use pesti-cides, so long as they are "organic pesticides."

The pesticide coating on seeds is absorbed into every part of the seedling and remains in the plant right up until harvesting. Even if the seedlings aren't exposed to further chemicals, the damage to treated seeds has already been done. It's far better to save your own untreated seeds so that you know there's no chance of consuming contaminated produce.

Helping Your Community

The middle class is under increasing pressure from the rising cost of food. As you grow your plants and vegeta-bles, it's important to remember that many people in your community are struggling to afford fresh food. You can help those less fortunate by gifting them some of your excess produce, or by selling extra vegetables at a price they can afford.

If possible, consider bartering fresh foods with your neighbors; such an arrangement will allow both of you access to a greater variety of vegetables than either one of you would ordinarily have on your own.

Invaluable Survival Skills for Preppers

The ultimate goal of prepping is to achieve total self-sufficiency. It means being able to take care of your own needs, such as food, water, shelter and any other human needs you may have without relying on outside help. In a world where pandemics, war and extreme weather events are becoming increasingly common, the need for people to be able to survive without depending on society has become greater than ever.

Food is one of the most vital elements for survival; it is essential in order to live a healthy life and maintain energy. Preppers understand that having a personal reserve of seeds gives them the opportunity to grow food on their own whenever needed. Having access to fresh produce can be a lifesaver if they're ever forced into a survival situation or when food shortages occur due to natural disasters.

Seed saving is an important skill and allows gardeners and preppers alike to ensure they'll always have access to healthy food no matter what happens. It's also incredibly rewarding; knowing that you can do it all yourself from seed collecting right through harvesting your crop gives you great satisfaction. So if you're looking for ways to increase your self-reliance, seed saving should definitely be part of your plan!

Chapter 2

Book II: Understanding Seeds and Their Life Cycle

Parts of a Seed

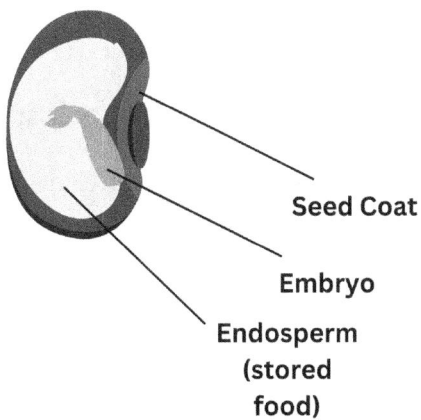

Seed Coat

Embryo

Endosperm
(stored
food)

A. Anatomy of a Seed: Structure and Function

Seeds are a wonder of nature. Within a hard shell, like the seed coat, is new life and the means to sustain life. Seeds are made up of three parts: the seed coat, which protects the embryo; the endosperm, which provides nutrients for growth; and finally the embryo itself, full of hope and promise.

Seed Coat:

The outer seed coat is hard and thick to protect the seed within from the ravages of nature. The seed coat functions to prevent moisture loss, helps to stop invasion by parasites and other small organisms, and protects it against environmental damage.

Endosperm:

The endosperm is an incredibly important part of the seed. Made up of protein, starch and oil, the endosperm stores food in reserve to feed the growing plant. The endosperm also acts as an extra layer of protection for the embryo within. In order to ensure that your seeds are adequately supplied with endosperm, it's important to pay attention to how well your plants are nourished during their growth cycle.

<u>Embryo:</u>

The embryo is like a baby plant inside the seed. The embryo contains the beginnings of all the parts that a plant needs to grow. For instance, it's made up of the tissues that will develop into the roots, leaves, and trunk of the plant. Like the endosperm, the embryo also contains food to sustain the seedling once it's planted.

There are two main parts of the embryo:

a. The first part is the baby plant's shoot. This part will develop by growing upward before turning into the stem and leaves of the plant.

b. The second part is the baby plant's root. This part will grow downward into the soil, where it can absorb nutrients and water for the plant.

B. Seed Formation and Maturation

The journey of a seed starts with the flowers of the mother plant, which hold its reproductive organs. The male flowers, or androecium, have the stamens located within their petals. Connected to each stamen is a thin stalk called a filament that leads up to a four-lobed organ called an anther. This anther creates pollen grains, and then bursts open when they are ready, releasing the pollen into the air.

The gynoecium, or female flower's, sex organs are called the pistil and are found in the middle of the flower. The ovary, at the base of the pistil, has a protruding stalk called a style, with a receptive tip called a stigma. The stigma takes in pollen which then germinates. Ovaries make one or several ovules. Ovules begin as a group of cells, or nucleus.

C. Pollination

In the pollination process, pollen from the male anther is delivered to the female stigma. In cross-pollination (pollination between two plants of the same species), pollination doesn't occur via direct transfer. Instead, many vectors are needed to move pollen from the male to the female flowers. Animals, wind, and water are just a few of the vectors responsible for carrying pollen to the female flower. Animal vectors are known as pollinators. Pollinators are often attracted to flowers for feeding purposes. When birds, bats, insects, and mammals feed from flowers, they unwittingly transfer pollen from plant to plant. In self-pollinating plants, there is no need for a vector because the plant can pollinate itself. This kind of pollination is possible when pollen lands from the anthers of a plant to the stigma of the same plant. During germination, a tube on the stigmata grows down until it reaches the ovule of the plant. The pollinated ovule then goes on to produce the seed.

D. Germination: The Process of Seed Sprouting

Seed germination isn't just a matter of placing the seed in soil and hoping for the best. A number of variables need to be just right before a seed will grow. Before a seed will germinate, conditions such as temperature, moisture, air and light have to be exact. For instance, if the temperature is too low or too high, a seed may die, or go into dormancy. Every seed has a minimum and maximum temperature threshold; anything beyond this will not allow for correct germination. Seeds need oxygen. For seeds to thrive, soil must be aerated enough to allow for air and water circulation. If the soil is too compact, it may suffocate the seedlings. Excessively soggy soil can also cause damage because the seeds can become waterlogged and unable to breathe. Achieving ideal moisture levels in soil is key to successful seed germination.

Seeds are programmed by nature to go dormant. If all seeds germinated at the same time, the risk of all being wiped out by an extreme weather event, for example, is high. Keeping some seeds dormant increases the chance of seeds germinating when conditions are more favorable. Unfortunately, this is not so useful for gardeners who want to germinate as many seeds as possible when planting them. Therefore, if seeds have entered a dormant state, they may need a little help to get going.

The method of triggering germination can be different for every seed. For instance, a seed with a thick and hard coat may need to be softened by soaking or ground down slightly. Some seeds respond to being frozen because cooler temperatures allow more oxygen in. Before attempting to break dormancy, it is best to research what actions will trigger germination in different seed types.

Ultimately, understanding these requirements is crucial for successful seed germination. For example, here are some common triggers for germination in different seed types:

Legumes (ex. beans, peas):

- Water: Legume seeds require adequate moisture to be able to initiate germination. If you soak the seeds overnight before you plant them, you can help kick-start the process.

- Temperature: Most legume seeds prefer soil temperatures around 70°F (21°C) for optimal germination.

Peppers (e.g., bell peppers, chili peppers, etc):

- Warmth: Pepper seeds tend to require warm soil temperatures if you want them to germinate successfully. It is ideal to use a temperature range of 75-85°F (24-29°C).

- Scarification: Some pepper varieties have tough seed coats. Scarification by lightly nicking the seed coat with a file or sandpaper can enhance germination rates.

Tomatoes:

- Warmth: Tomato seeds will require warm temperatures between 70-85°F (21-29°C) for germination.

- Light: Tomato seeds are negatively photoblastic, meaning they germinate better in darkness. Sow tomato seeds at a depth where they receive little to no light.

Melons (e.g., watermelon, cantaloupe):

- Warmth: Melon seeds thrive in warm soil temperatures around 75-85°F (24-29°C) for successful germination.

- Scarification: Some melon seeds have hard seed coats. Soaking them in water overnight or lightly sanding the seed coat can help improve germination rates.

Keep in mind that these are just general guidelines. In fact, specific varieties within each seed type may have slightly different requirements. So always be sure to check with reliable gardening references for accurate and detailed germination information specific on the seeds you are working with, for optimal results.

How to Germinate Seeds

For most seeds, water is the primary trigger for germination. So if you want to get the process of germination going, you will need water and plenty of it. When the seed becomes moistened, the seed coat will soften, allowing water to penetrate it and initiate the germination process.

Initially, it will appear as if nothing is happening. You may not see any changes in the soil for days! But, don't fear. There's plenty going on that you can't see. During what may seem like an inactive stage, the seed is activating internal processes to begin germination. The cells take in more oxygen. The seed starts to use its food stores to make protein. The main root, called a radical, will emerge from the seed coat.

The radical immediately begins to take in the water, allowing for the shoot to push its way to the surface. Then the first leaves emerge. Meanwhile, the roots branch out deeper into the soil. It's important that seeds develop slowly and evenly at this stage. Ensure that the soil is always moist, but not too moist, to prevent the seeds from damping off. How often you water can depend on a number of factors. If the temperature is high, water will evaporate more quickly, causing the soil to dry out. Some people prefer to water every second day to prevent overwatering. It's best to check daily to make sure the plant is kept moist but not pooled with water. The soil should feel wet and should look puddled. If the soil is loose or separates and looks dry, you'll need to add more water.

It is more beneficial to water from below. This method allows the roots of the plant to absorb the moisture they need, as opposed to just wetting the topsoil. If you water from the top, the water may not be able to reach past the topsoil and get enough hydration deep into the soil to nourish the roots.

Chapter 3

Book III: Choose the Right Plants for Seed Saving Like an Expert

Seed Types and Differences: Open-Pollinated, Heirloom, and Hybrid Seeds: Definitions and Differences

<u>Open-Pollinated</u>

In this method of propagation, different organisms like insects, birds, wind, and water act as vectors in pollination. Open-pollinated plants boast a wider array of gene types, since pollination is random. This genetic diversity increases their adaptability to the climate in their area. Furthermore, the grower can pick out a plant with desirable characteristics and save its seed so that they can reproduce the same desired qualities in the next growing season.

Heirloom Seeds

Just as some families pass heirloom jewelry, paintings and furniture down to new generations, so, too, do plant families share seeds with the next generation. These seeds are selected based on certain traits they possess, and they are saved to pass on to younger family members to use. Heirloom seeds use open-pollination to reproduce. Many companies classify seeds as belonging to the heirloom variety if the seed is more than 50 years old. And, some seed savers are even more meticulous regarding their classification of heirloom seeds, requiring a documented history of the seeds being passed on from one grower to another.

Hybrid Seeds

Hybrid plants are created when two different parent plants are cross-pollinated to produce offspring, a third plant, with specific and desirable traits. Essentially, hybridization aims to combine the best traits of each parent, such as disease resistance, uniformity, or productivity. Hybridization can also occur naturally. Deliberate hybridization, known as F1, has specifically chosen traits, such as resistance to disease, bred into them. Some gardeners, who seek specific traits, such as disease resistance or high yields, may choose hybrids for their consistent performance. However, it should be noted that hybrid plants do not produce stable offspring from saved seeds. If the seeds are saved and replanted, the resulting plants tend to exhibit unpredictable traits.

How They Compare:

The advantage of heirloom and open-pollinated seeds is that they have greater genetic diversity, making them more adaptable to environmental conditions like temperature. If an environment is different from that in which a hybrid seed was grown in, the hybrid plant might not do as well as the two, more adaptable varieties.

The advantage of using heirloom seeds instead of open-pollinated seeds is that you can rest in the knowledge that the plants you are growing have a long history of success. As well, it's a deeply satisfying feeling to know that you are using trusted, and natural seeds that have been successful for generations of gardeners before you.

Meanwhile, hybrid plants tend to grow and produce better than the plants they were bred from, due to an occurrence known as hybrid 'vigor.' However, seeds that come from hybrid plants are genetically unstable and tend to be inferior to the seeds of open-pollinated and heirloom seeds. This is why growers who use these seeds tend to need to purchase seeds every year.

B. Plant Isolation Techniques to Keep Genetic Seed Purity

Plant isolation is essential if you want to keep your plant from being pollinated by another plant of the same species that you don't intend to cross with. Isolation is essential in order to prevent your crop's genetics from being contaminated.

<u>How to Isolate Plants</u>

Use time to isolate two plants of the same species by planting one much earlier than the other. Only plant the second type once the first has fully pollinated and produced seeds.

Physical barriers are also a good way of isolating plants. Using paper, cloth bags, and mesh will prevent pollination. You may also plant very thick rows of flowers between the plants you don't want cross-pollinating. You could use separate hydroponic units, or glass houses.

With enough distance, you should be able to prevent plants from pollinating with unwanted neighbors. Be sure to investigate the distance needed for different plant types.

C. Choosing the Best Plants for Seed Saving

There are many considerations to take into account when choosing seeds for saving. Vigor is an important consideration; you want a plant that will grow quickly and produce well. If you're planting an heirloom variety, it's best to choose one that has all of the features showing the main characteristics of the plant. Disease, insect resistance, tolerance to drought, and excess moisture are all good things to look for when choosing seeds. Size, shape, and flavor are all important factors when deciding whether a plant is a good one for harvesting seeds from. No one wants a bland-tasting, colorless crop.

Which Plant Types to Save Seeds From

When choosing which plants to collect seeds from, it's good to strike a balance between the plants you want and how easy they are to save and grow. Some plants are more delicate and may not survive environmental factors like fluctuations in temperature. Some take more care than others.

Peppers, beans, peas, lettuce, artichoke, and tomatoes are great choices for seed saving because their flowers self-pollinate. They're also easy to deal with, needing little treatment before storage.

Biennial crops need two seasons before they will seed. Carrots, cauliflower, turnips, onions, and beets are examples of plants that need two growing seasons. That means it will take two years before you can harvest and collect seeds. After the first year, biennials go dormant. A cold period is often needed in order to bring these plants out of dormancy. Sometimes they will need artificial treatment with cold temperatures before they will flower. Because of the time it takes to flower and seed, these crops are more time-consuming and difficult to work with. However, biennials that are harvested for leaves are ideal. Parsley, and other leafy greens, for instance, can be harvested for leaves in the first year.

When it comes to fruit, melon seeds are excellent for saving. Melons typically require only one growing season to reach maturity and produce fruit. Of course, the length of the growing season for melons will vary depending on the specific variety and environmental conditions.

On average, melon plants take approximately 70 to 90 days from seed sowing to harvest. It's important to note that melons are warm-season crops and require warm soil and air temperatures to thrive. They are typically planted in the spring after the danger of frost has passed and can be harvested during the summer months.

The exact timing of growth stages and fruit maturity will also depend on the specific melon variety. Some melon varieties may have shorter growing seasons, while others may take longer to mature. Additionally, factors such as sunlight, soil fertility, water availability, and proper care practices can influence the overall growth and productivity of melon plants.

Monitoring the development of the fruit is key. Melons are typically harvested when they reach their full size, exhibit the desired color or pattern, have a slight give when gently pressed, and emit a sweet aroma. Checking the specific instructions provided with the chosen melon variety or consulting local gardening resources can help determine the estimated growing season and harvest timing for successful melon cultivation in your specific region.

D. Which Seeds to Avoid Saving

It's best to avoid hybrids and cross-pollinators as both are likely to result in disappointing crops.

Hybrid seeds are usually only good for a single season. Typically, seeds from a hybrid plant always produce inferior plants. A plant from a hybrid seed will produce either the original parent plants, or it could form something else entirely. If it falls into the latter category, then it will likely still be edible but not necessarily tasty. Overall, it's simply not worth the time and energy trying to take seeds from a hybrid, when the results are likely to be unsatisfying.

It's hard to predict what will result from the crops of cross-pollinated seeds, and the outcome is not likely to be what is intended. What's more, cross-pollinated plants can cross with other members of the same species. For instance, given that broccoli, brussel sprouts and cabbage are all from the Brassica family, you can see how cross-pollinating these plants could result in something unpredictable. The problem with cross-pollination is that it means the resulting seed is unlikely to be true to type - or like the plant you took the seed from. Cross-pollination also poses problems in maintaining genetic integrity because the resultant seeds can deviate significantly from the parent plant you wish to proliferate.

E. Least Successful Seeds for Storage

Some plants don't store so well and have a short life in storage. Parsnips and alliums (onion family: leeks, shallots, scallions) lose 50% of their germination each year, no matter how well stored they are. This is why you should try to choose plants that can last for many years, and are not too complicated to care for when it comes to storage.

Chapter 4

Book IV: Easy Seed Harvesting – Learn the Secrets to Effectively Collecting Seeds

A. Identifying Seed Maturity: Signs and Techniques

One of the most crucial aspects of seed saving is knowing when the seeds have reached maturity. The timing of seed harvesting is a delicate process. If seeds are harvested too early, they'll be small and shriveled and the embryo won't be fully formed, so the seed probably won't germinate. Seeds that are left too long to develop may pre-germinate inside the pod. The best time to harvest is just when the embryo is mature, but before the seeds start to pre-germinate.

Properly identifying seed maturity ensures that you collect seeds at the optimal time, increasing the chances of successful germination in future seasons. Here are some signs to look for when determining seed maturity for different types of plants.

General Seed Maturity Signs

Seeds go through visible changes as they mature. Observing these signs can help you identify the right time for seed collection:

Color Change: As seeds mature, they often undergo a noticeable color transformation. Keep an eye out for changes from vibrant green to brown, black, or specific hues associated with the particular plant variety. This color shift is a reliable indicator of seed maturity.

Dry and Hard Seed Coat: Mature seeds develop a dry and hard outer coat, protecting them from moisture and environmental factors. When you gently press a mature seed, it should feel firm and resistant.

Seed Separation: In some cases, mature seeds naturally separate from their surrounding structures. For example, seeds may detach from pods or fruit pulp as they reach full maturity. Keep an eye out for this separation, as it signifies that the seeds are ready for collection.

Vegetable Seeds

Saving seeds from vegetables requires careful attention to their maturity. Look for the following signs to determine when vegetable seeds are ready for harvesting:

1. Full Size and Weight: Vegetable seeds, such as those found in tomatoes, cucumbers, or peppers, should attain their full size and feel heavier when mature. Take note of their growth and weight to gauge their maturity level accurately.

2. Fruit Ripeness: Harvest vegetables when they have fully ripened. In most cases, this is the ideal time for seed collection, as the mature fruit contains seeds that are ready to be saved.

Herb Seeds

Herbs provide an abundance of flavorful leaves and also produce seeds. Here's how to recognize seed maturity in herbs:

1. Drying of Flower Heads: Many herbs, including

basil, cilantro, or dill, develop seeds after their flower heads have dried and turned brown. Keep a close eye on the flower heads, as their drying is a reliable signal that the seeds are maturing.

2. Melon Seeds: Melon seeds reach maturity when the fruit itself is fully ripe. It's essential to allow the melon to fully develop on the vine until it exhibits all the characteristics of ripeness. Depending on the variety, this may include a change in color, such as turning yellow, orange, or exhibiting a vibrant hue associated with the specific melon type.

Seed Cavity Appearance: When you cut open a ripe melon, observe the seeds and the surrounding flesh. The seeds should appear plump, mature, and well-formed. Immature seeds are usually soft, pale, or underdeveloped.

Slippery Texture: In some melon varieties, the fruit stem or the area connecting the fruit to the vine will naturally detach or become loose when the melon is ripe. This "slip" indicates that the melon is mature and ready for harvest, including the seeds inside.

Remember, the signs of seed maturity can vary between plant species and varieties. It's always beneficial to consult reliable seed-saving references or resources that offer specific guidance for the plants you are working with. A general rule you can follow is that testing by eye is a good way of judging when seeds are ready.

Typically, seeds that are mature will have a hardened seed coat and darkened color. Pearly or translucent seeds are too young to harvest and probably won't germinate. Darkening seeds are nearing maturity. When the seed turns dark and hard, they are ready to harvest. Check seeds daily and take the ones which appear mature. Generally, seeds on the lowest point on the plant should be the first to mature, so keep a close eye on these for signs of maturation.

B. Essential Seed Harvesting Tools and Equipment

Tools for Wet Seeds

Wet seeds come from inside fruit and vegetables. The gel surrounding the seeds needs to be removed by fermentation, which entails placing seeds into a container, like a mason jar, a preserving jar or other container until the debris separates from the seed.

Tools for Dry Seed Harvest

When it comes to harvesting seeds from dry varieties, you'll need a few tools in order to get the job done. One of the most important pieces of equipment is a seed screen, which is used to separate the seeds from any chaff (debris) that may be stuck to them. A seed screen is essentially a fine mesh sieve that allows you to sift out the chaff and collect only the viable seeds. Additionally, you can use a manual thresher or combine harvester for larger scale seed collecting projects.

Drying and Storage Tools

Once you have collected and cleaned your seeds, the next step in creating a successful seed bank is to dry them. Drying your seeds before storing them will help ensure that they are viable for longer periods of time. You can use several tools to dry out your seeds—which is best for you may depend on how much time you have and what kind of drying environment you're working with.

If you're looking for a quick-drying solution, a food dehydrator is an easy way to speed up the process; however, make sure that you use the lowest temperature setting to avoid the risk of accidentally cooking your seeds. Dehydrating seeds can take anywhere between 20-30 minutes. Other popular drying tools include parchment paper (for slow drying), screens (which will help keep out pests), and mesh bags (to allow for better airflow around the seeds).

As for storage, you have many options to safely stockpile your seeds, and none of them will break the bank, which is great considering we are building a seed bank! For instance, you can store your seeds inside of a coin envelope, or zip lock bag.

Proper container for long-term storage: Select appropriate containers for storing your seeds. You can use airtight and moisture-resistant containers such as glass jars, metal tins, or plastic containers with tight-fitting lids. Avoid using containers that may leach harmful chemicals or allow moisture to enter.

Consider Desiccant Packs or Silica Gel: To further protect against moisture, you can add desiccant packs or silica gel to your storage containers. These help to absorb excess moisture and maintain a dry environment for the seeds.

Create Ideal Storage Conditions: Store your seeds in a cool, dry, and dark location. Ideally, the temperature should be consistently cool (around 32-41°F or 0-5°C), with low humidity levels (below 50%). Avoid storing seeds in areas prone to temperature fluctuations, such as attics or garages.

A refrigerator or freezer can be suitable for long-term storage, as long as the seeds are properly sealed in moisture-proof packaging.

The most important thing in choosing your storage container is to make sure the seeds are sealed away in an airtight, moisture-free container and kept in a dark place.

C. When to Collect Your Seeds

Seeds are ready to collect when they change color from green to brown, red or black. It never hurts to refer to resources about the seed you are harvesting so you will be aware of its expected maturation color. If you're harvesting seeds for a plant for the first time, do some research to see what changes occur to the seed as it matures. For instance, when peas are immature, they will look pale or translucent. Approaching maturity, they will become greener. When ready for harvest, they will appear brown.

Here are a few more examples of vegetables and herbs and when their seeds are ready for collection.

Vegetables

Tomatoes: Harvest tomatoes for seed saving when they are fully ripe. Look for signs of maturity, such as a rich color and a slightly soft texture. Avoid harvesting tomatoes that are still green or underripe, as the seeds inside may not have fully developed.

Peppers: Collect pepper seeds when the peppers have reached their desired level of ripeness. Most pepper varieties change color as they mature, transitioning from green to yellow, orange, red, or other specific hues. Wait until the peppers have fully changed color before harvesting and extracting the seeds.

Cucumbers: For seed saving, allow cucumbers to remain on the vine until they are fully mature. The cucumbers should reach their typical size and develop a firm texture. Avoid picking cucumbers when they are small or still developing, as their seeds may not be fully developed.

Herbs

Basil: Harvest basil seeds when the plant has produced its flowers and the flower heads have begun to dry out. When the flower head begins to brown and turns brittle, then at this stage the seeds within the flowers will be mature and ready for collection.

Cilantro: When saving cilantro seeds, wait until the plant has flowered and the flowers have transitioned into seed heads. Once the seed heads dry and turn brown, they will start to split open. This will indicate that the seeds are mature and can be collected.

Dill: Collect dill seeds when the plant's umbels (flower clusters) have dried and turned brown. The seeds will be ready for harvesting when they easily detach from the umbels with a gentle touch. Make sure to collect the seeds before they disperse naturally.

By observing these guidelines and understanding the specific signs of maturity for each vegetable and herb, you can accurately determine when to collect seeds for optimal quality and viability.

D. Challenges and Solutions when Choosing and Collecting Seeds

Challenges When Choosing Seeds

When it comes to choosing the right seeds for your garden, sometimes it seems you can't win. You might find yourself trying different seed varieties season after season, only to notice that they don't germinate or have low seed yields. One of the most important considerations in choosing seeds is to *match your seeds to your environment.*

If you live in a particularly warm region, it is wise to choose seeds that are suited to warm conditions. Plants like sweet peppers, okra, eggplant, hot peppers, and tomatoes are just a few of the many plants which thrive in warm conditions. If you leave somewhere with wet conditions, likewise, you should choose plants that do well in wetter environments. Asparagus, taro, cabbage, watercress and celery are some of the plants that thrive in wet soil conditions. If you wish to grow produce during colder times, choose plants that can withstand the cold, such as spinach, peas, and kale.

Spinach – Spinach is cold-hardy and can survive temperatures as low as 20 degrees F. These rapidly growing veggies are best suited for fall gardening. This means that, ideally, they should be planted in mid-August to mid-September. Before the first frost hits, they should have at least 6 weeks of growth. Most spinach varieties can take up 37 - 45 days to go from being sown to reaching full maturity.

Peas – Peas are cold-resistant legumes, able to withstand frost. However, they struggle in hot weather. The soil should be worked as soon as possible for these cold-loving legumes. Planting pea seeds in the spring will guarantee that they'll have enough time to reach maturity before the hot summer months arrive.

Kale – This leafy green vegetable grows easily and can tolerate cold climates. For colder regions, start seedlings indoors before transplanting them outdoors a month before frost-free weather arrives. Start harvesting leaves when your plants reach about 8 inches in height.

The area you live in might be prone to particular pests. For instance, if you are trying to grow tomatoes in a region that has a known tomato hornworm problem, it may be wise to choose varieties designed to withstand these pests. For example, the *Husky Cherry Red* cherry tomato is known for its strong resistance to hornworms, which makes it a popular choice for home gardeners. *Jasper* cherry tomatoes are also recognized for their resistance to hornworms, as well as other common tomato pests, like aphids and whiteflies.

Alternatively, if you live in an area that is rife with a certain pest that targets specific plants, you may choose to grow a different plant entirely.

Challenges When Collecting Seeds

Not having enough seeds is a huge problem that many home gardeners, who want to save their own seeds, can face at the start of their journey. A lack of seeds can slow down your seed bank plans or halt them entirely. There are many reasons you can struggle to collect seeds. For instance, some plants may be sterile or have only male parts, so collecting seeds from these won't be fruitful. Another reason is that seed production is draining for a plant. Plants may skip a season to shore up reserves. This can happen if growth has been disrupted by environmental challenges like drought or heavy rainfall. It's important to have enough plants, spread out in different areas to overcome issues that slow seed production.

Some seeds aren't viable, and won't germinate when planted. A number of factors, such as the state of seeds when they were collected, may result in inviable seeds. Harvesting too early or too late can also be to blame. Take note of when you harvest your seeds, keep a calendar if needed, and experiment with harvesting a bit sooner or later next time to see if this helps with future crop viability.

Unfortunately, some seeds are more challenging to collect than others. We encourage beginner home-gardeners to start with plants that are easier to collect seeds from. For instance, carrot seeds are small and may be hard to find. It makes more sense to start with larger seeds from plants that are beginner -friendly and grow easily in a single season. Here are just a few examples of fool-proof vegetables and herbs you can start with, and easily collect seeds from for abundant yields in the future, even as a novice.

Radishes: Radishes are quick-growing root vegetables that are perfect for beginners. They mature in just a few weeks, making them a satisfying choice for those looking for fast results. Radishes can be grown in both spring and fall and require minimal space and care.

Basil: Basil is a versatile herb that thrives in warm weather. It is easy to grow from seeds or transplants and provides an abundant harvest throughout the summer. With its aromatic leaves, basil adds a flavorful touch to countless dishes and can be used in pesto, salads, and sauces.

Zucchini: Zucchini is a prolific summer squash that is known for its easy cultivation and abundant yields. It grows quickly and produces an abundance of delicious squash that can be enjoyed in various recipes. Zucchini plants appreciate full sun and regular watering.

Lettuce: Lettuce is a versatile and fast-growing leafy green that can be harvested at various stages, from baby greens to full heads. It is easy to grow from seeds or transplants and thrives in cooler temperatures. With a variety of colors and textures available, lettuce is a great addition to salads and sandwiches.

Sunflowers: Sunflowers are iconic and low-maintenance flowers that are perfect for beginner gardeners. They grow tall and produce vibrant, sun-like blooms that bring beauty to any garden. Sunflowers thrive in full sun and well-draining soil. Plus, they can be grown from seeds directly in the ground.

Green Beans: Green beans, also called snap beans or string beans, are a popular choice for home gardens. They are fairly easy to grow and they produce abundant yields. Green beans come in bush or pole varieties and can be harvested when the pods are tender and crisp. They thrive in warmer weather and full sun.

These plants will provide you with a wonderful, bountiful starting point. They offer not only simplicity, but satisfyingly fast growth, and a rewarding harvest all in the span of a single season! Go ahead and experiment with these plants to build your confidence, and lay the foundation for more ambitious gardening endeavors in the future as you gain more practice and skill in the art of seed-saving and growing.

E. Expert Techniques for Properly Extracting Seeds from Different Plants

Perennial seeds and annual seeds are ready for harvest when the petals have fallen off of the flowers. At this stage, it's time to collect the seeds. Begin by cutting the head of the flower with scissors or by knife. Place the ripe seeds on the paper or other medium of your choice, and set them aside to dry. Once dry, remove any pods, husks or other debris from the seed. Use gloves when removing debris to avoid transferring moisture from your hands to the seed. Place the seeds in a paper envelope and then place them in an airtight container somewhere that's cool, dark, and dry.

When it comes to saving seeds from fruits and vegetables, a different approach for specific kinds may be needed. For beans and peas, it's easy to see when it's harvest time because the pods will turn brown and start to open. To harvest, remove seeds from the dried pods, and dry out as usual.

When it comes to cucumber and tomato seeds, remove the pulp and seeds, and place in a container with water until fermentation is complete. The dead seeds will rise, the viable seeds will drop to the bottom. Then remove the pulp and clean the seeds for drying out and then storage.

For peppers, wait until the fruit is fully ripe and firm to the touch. The peppers should have developed their mature color. Choose only from the healthiest plants. and starting to wrinkle. Remove the seeds from the middle and dry as usual. Cut open the pepper using a sharp knife to carefully slice it lengthwise from stem to tip. Be cautious of the pepper's heat level and wear gloves if handling hot peppers to avoid skin irritation.

To remove the seeds, hold the pepper over a bowl or a clean surface and gently scrape the seeds from the pepper's inner walls using a spoon or your fingers. Try to separate as many seeds as possible from the flesh of the pepper.

Clean the seeds by placing the collected seeds in a sieve or fine-mesh strainer. Rinse them under cool running water to remove any remaining flesh or debris. Gently shake the sieve to help separate the seeds from the water. Finally, dry the seeds in the method you desire. We suggest spreading the cleaned seeds in a single layer on a paper towel or a clean, dry plate. Then, place them in a well-ventilated area away from direct sunlight. Allow the seeds to dry completely for about one to two weeks. Ensure they are fully dry before storing to prevent mold or rot.

With watermelons, all you need to do is remove the seeds from the pulp, and rinse in a strainer before drying. When saving watermelon seeds, it's essential to allow the fruits to fully ripen on the vine. Then, scoop out the seeds, separate the seeds from the pulp, rinse thoroughly and let them air dry in a cool, well-ventilated area. Be sure to choose a variety that will produce seeds for future generations. These include open-pollinated or heirloom watermelon varieties, because they typically produce seeds that will grow true to their parent plants, allowing you to save them for up to four years, and sow them when you are ready.

A few examples of open-pollinated watermelon varieties that are suitable for seed saving include the 'Sugar Baby,' popular heirloom variety. 'Sugar Baby' is a small, round watermelon with sweet, juicy flesh. It is known for its early maturity and compact size, making it suitable for smaller gardens. 'Moon and Stars,' an heirloom watermelon variety, that features dark green skin with yellow spots, resembling a night sky dotted with stars. 'Moon and Stars' produces sweet, red flesh and can grow to a larger size, making it a favorite among home gardeners. And, 'Blacktail Mountain,' an open-pollinated variety, prized for its ability to thrive in cooler climates. It produces small to medium-sized melons with sweet, red flesh. 'Blacktail Mountain' is known for its early maturity and excellent flavor.

Chapter 5

Book V: Seed Cleaning and Processing

A. The Importance of Seed Cleaning: Removing Debris and Inert Matter

The main goal of seed cleaning is to remove debris without causing damage to, or loss of, the seed. Seed cleaning is more important than you might think. Your crops will have greater longevity, health and success in germinating if they're clean before being stored. If you don't remove debris and inert material, your seeds might become moist and rot from the outside. If diseased seeds aren't separated before storing, the disease, mold, or fungi that has destroyed bad seeds might spread to healthy ones. Thereby, destroying a large amount of your seed bank.

B. Best Seed Cleaning Methods and Tools

Tools Needed For Cleaning

You will need the following tools for cleaning a variety of seeds:

- Dust mask
- Aspirator
- gloves
- Stainless steel sieves with a variety of mesh sizes
- Wire brush
- Small bristle brushes
- trays
- Forceps
- Scalpel or knife
- Paper packets and fasteners

Best Seed Cleaning Techniques

There are four techniques for cleaning a seeds

1. Using sieves to separate seeds from bulk material and smaller debris.

2. Hand-sorting to remove debris bit by bit from the seed.

3. Using a seed aspirator to remove lighter seeds from heavier ones, which separates empty, dead or infest-

ed/diseased seeds from healthy seeds.

4. Using a rubber mat to finger-rub debris away more
   gently.

Sieving

One of the most commonly used methods of seed clean-ing, sieving, entails separating the seed from debris by al-lowing the seed to pass through the mesh hole, leaving the debris behind.

You will need a variety of sieves with different-sized holes depending on the size of the seeds you are using. The holes should be big enough to allow the seeds to fall out without being damaged, but not so big that debris comes through. To use, place a handful of seeds on the sieve and gently rub with your fingers until as many seeds have fallen through the holes as possible. Check the debris for leftover seeds, and discard when you cannot find any seeds left behind.

If you find that some of the seeds have been damaged after passing through the sieve, you should experiment with another method of cleaning, as this one may be too harsh.

Hand-Sorting

Cleaning by hand is best when seeds are relatively clean, as otherwise, it can be a lengthy process. Place seeds on a flat surface, like a plate, and gently remove any debris by hand. Visually separate viable seeds from empty, damaged ones. If you find it's taking too long or there is more debris than expected, you may wish to try cleaning by sieve.

Aspirator

An aspirator is used to separate lighter materials from desired seeds during cleaning and sorting. It uses airflow to carry away debris, while allowing the heavier seeds to be collected. This helps improve seed purity and quality, particularly for small seeds or those mixed with impurities. Proper adjustment of airflow and screen settings is crucial for effective seed separation.

When it comes to selecting seeds for aspirator-assisted cleaning and sorting, it is beneficial to choose seeds that are relatively larger and have a distinct weight and density compared to the accompanying debris. A few examples of seeds that generally respond well to aspirator-based seed cleaning include beans, peas, sunflowers, and corn.

If there is a lot of unwanted material on your seed, put them through a sieve before an aspirator. If the seeds are relatively clean, you can place them straight into an aspirator. And remaining empty seeds and light debris will be separated from your seeds.

To begin, place seeds in the hopper of the aspirator. The airflow setting will need to be sufficient to remove light, dead seeds, and unwanted material from the seed. Use trial and error to determine if enough of the debris and unviable seeds are being lifted away. If there are a lot of seeds remaining in the rubbish, open some of the seeds up to check whether healthy seeds have been discarded. If there are too many bad seeds, return them to the aspirator and set it to a lower blow setting. If, after several attempts, there is too much dead seed or debris remaining, sort by hand or sieve.

Fleshy Seeds

Mature seeds within fleshy fruit or vegetables can over-mature quickly, so try to remove them in a timely manner. Many fruit seeds may be toxic, so you may consider wearing gloves when handling them. Open the fruit with a knife, or use your fingers to remove seeds and pulp and place them onto a sieve. Due to the amount of fruit material, running the sieve through water may be required to allow the seeds to fall through. Wash away the pulp in warm water.

C. Seed Storage Techniques

Now that your seeds have been cleaned and dried, it is time to store them. The following expert tips will help you learn how to effectively store your seeds for months or even years, even if you are a beginner.

To effectively store seeds it is paramount that you keep your seeds dry. Moisture is the enemy of seed storage, because it can lead to mold, decay, and loss of viability. That is why it is so important to properly and thoroughly dry your seeds before storing them. Remember, you can use a moisture-absorbing desiccant packet or include a dry paper towel in the storage container to help maintain low humidity levels.

You want to store your seeds in airtight containers to not only protect them from moisture, but excess air, and pests. Glass jars with tight-fitting lids or sealed plastic bags are commonly used for seed storage. Ensure that the containers are clean, dry, and free from any residual odors that could affect seed quality.

Store in a cool, dark, and stable environment, since temperature and light can also impact seed longevity. Choose a storage location that is cool (around 32-41°F or 0-5°C), dark, and free from temperature fluctuations. Avoid storing seeds in areas prone to extreme heat, such as attics or near appliances. In fact, you may consider refrigeration or freezing. This is especially true for long-term storage. Place seeds in airtight containers or sealed bags, and store them away in a refrigerator or freezer. This method can extend seed viability for many years! However, it's important to note that not all seeds tolerate freezing well, so research the specific requirements for each seed type.

It is important to routinely monitor stored seeds to ensure they remain dry and free from any signs of moisture or pests. If condensation forms inside the container, remove the seeds, dry them thoroughly, and consider new storage containers.

Chapter 6

Book VI. Seed Drying and Storage by Plant Type

A. The Best Conditions and Techniques For Storing - Seed Drying

Because seeds will germinate when wet and hibernate when dry, so seeds must be as dry as possible for storage. Open-air drying is the easiest way to dry, and it can be just as successful as any other technique. In fact, it's possible to successfully dry seeds with everyday items. Even when seeds dry out on the plant, they may contain a lot of moisture from dew or rain. Seeds may feel dry, but they aren't dry enough. First, they need to be separated and dried in the air. Even when seeds seem extra dry, when they've been harvested during warm, sunny weather, for instance, they still require extra drying. Skipping the drying process will result in moldy seeds.

In order to achieve optimal drying, air-dried seeds need to have air on each seed. Sieves are the best way to ensure enough air gets to your seeds. You don't need to spend a lot of money. You may have something at home that will do the job. Window screens, salad spinners, or strainers can all work as long as the holes are small enough. If seeds are wet to begin with, such as fruit seeds, they will need to be dried within three days, or they'll sprout.

For best results, stir your seeds to ensure even drying and to break up any seeds that are too close. If you feel like your seeds aren't drying well, you can use a fan to get the air moving around the room. As a last resort, apply heat as in from food dehydrators. Though it may take practice to ensure seeds aren't overheated and destroyed.

Some people dry seeds out on paper, like paper towels. However, seeds can sometimes stick to ordinary paper towels. Parchment paper or waxed paper is better to avoid seeds sticking.

B. Long-Term Storage Techniques to Build a Seed Bank That Last Years and Factors Affecting Seed Viability

Light, temperature and moisture are the three most important things that you need to manage when it comes to long-term seed storage.

Light

Light can spur your seeds into sprouting, so it's best to keep your seeds as far away from light as possible. If you store seeds in mason jars or other see-through containers, make sure these are then stored in a dark place. Anything that blocks out the light will suffice for storing your seed containers. A cupboard, drawers, filing cabinets, or solid boxes are a few examples of good storage places.

Temperature

Temperature is another environmental cue that will bring about germination. Different seeds are spurred into sprouting by different temperatures, but as a general rule, keeping temperatures below 40 degrees Fahrenheit should be enough. If you find your seeds don't fare well at this temperature, you will need to lower the temperature further.

Freezing seeds is optimal. However, power cuts may lead to seeds thawing, resulting in rotting. If you have to store seeds at room temperature, try to keep the temperature even. Sudden hikes in temperature may mimic spring conditions when seeds naturally germinate.

Moisture

Without water, seeds likely wouldn't germinate. With it, they are very likely to do so. Keeping moisture away from your seeds is a priority. Keeping your containers airtight is essential. Zip lock bags are effective in keeping the wet at bay. Jars and plastic containers are also good at keeping moisture out as long as the seals are airtight. When using paper envelopes, it's even more important to keep them dry as moisture from wet paper is more easily transferred to the seed. Popping powdered milk, rice, or silica into your seed container will also help to soak up any extra moisture.

By following these professional seed-storing techniques, you'll be able to maximize the longevity and viability of your stored seeds, thereby creating a reliable seed bank of well-preserved seeds that you can use for months or even years to come.

Pro Tip: Seed Viability

Different seed types remain viable for longer than others. All organic materials break down over time, and seeds are no different, no matter how efficiently you have stored them. When saving seeds, it's good to know when to expect to see signs of seed decay.

Seeds that should last 1-2 years include chives, parsnip, pepper, shallot, garlic, leek, onion, parsley and sweet corn.

Seeds that should last 3-4 years include celery, eggplant, peas, squash, tomatoes, watermelon, asparagus, beans, broccoli, brussels sprouts, cabbage, carrots, and cauliflower.

Seeds that should last 5-6 years include lettuce, radish, cucumber, basil, mustard greens, and endive.

Seeds can begin to degrade at any time. It pays to do a germination test every now and then. To do a germination test, place seeds inside two pieces of dampened paper. Check within a week to see if the seeds have germinated.

Some seeds, like peas, can be placed in a bowl of water. If a seed floats, that means they are not viable.

C. Packing and Storage: Choosing the Right Containers, and/or Packaging Materials

Store seeds in a labeled envelope, and be sure to include a label with the date, so you know when the seeds will lose viability. After that, the seeds need to be placed in an airtight environment. You can use any container including mason jars, jam jars, plastic containers, and cookie tins, for example. A pill box is a good idea if you want to store a variety of seeds in one place. The main thing is that the container is airtight. If you really want to ensure that your seeds are well protected, consider purchasing a container with a vacuum seal. Placing a material that absorbs moisture into your seed envelope will ensure any rogue moisture is quickly removed. Silica, cat litter, and rice are a few good examples.

Make sure humidity is below 8 percent moisture, and below 40 degrees Fahrenheit, and your seeds will stand the best chance of surviving. Freezing is the best choice. As long as there's no power failure, freezing will keep seeds at a uniform temperature.

The best place for storing seeds is one that remains constant in temperature and humidity. A basement is a good choice, as it will be less likely to heat up in the summer. Basements tend to be dark and cool despite the temperature outside. As long as moisture is controlled, a basement will suffice for storage of seeds. If your basement is damp, using a dehumidifier daily will help to take out any dampness.

D. Storage Advice You Need to Know: Common Issues, and Solutions

What can you do if pests, such as weevils, mice or ants have gotten into your seed store? Pest invasion is likely to happen if your method of storing isn't robust. If you store your seeds in paper envelopes, it's easy for pests to gain access to your precious seed harvest. Plastic bags are not enough to keep some pests at bay either. Although a sealed plastic bag will certainly keep moisture and air out, they offer little protection against rodents. You will need to place your seeds in something more robust, such as plastic containers.

What if you've followed all the best advice on storing seeds, and your seeds still germinate? If you manage to make sure light, heat, and air have been kept away from your seeds, there are still a few reasons why your seeds may not have germinated. You might've harvested them too late, meaning germination was already in progress before you stored your seeds. Your seeds may not have been dried out properly before storage. Therefore, moisture in the seeds was enough to facilitate germination.

What if your seeds keep expiring before you want to plant them? You may not have organized your seeds properly. If you store different seasons' seeds close together, there's a chance you may mix up older seeds with newer ones. To avoid this mistake, always label your seeds with dates. Place older seeds in front of newer ones as a way to encourage you to use them first. Your seeds may not have been viable in the first place. Always do thorough viability tests before storing seeds. You should even carry out viability tests on your stored seeds from time to time.

What if your seeds go moldy? Mold tends to indicate that your seeds did not dry out enough before storage. To avoid this, check your seeds periodically to test for signs of sweating, which include condensation on jars and dampness in your packaging. Immediately take steps to dry out your seeds the way you would before storing. Do not wait if you see signs of moisture, as this means your seeds will go moldy quickly.

What if you did everything right and your seeds don't germinate? Your germination techniques may be to blame, not the way in which you've stored them. If you did everything right in terms of seed storage, it may be that you've over-watered or under-watered your seeds.

Chapter 7

Book VII. Establishing and Managing a Seed Bank

A. Organizing and Cataloging Your Seed Collection

The better organized and cataloged your seed collection is, the easier it will be for you when it comes time to plant. If you're planting seeds for your personal use, you can use a storage container that has different compartments, such as a pill box. This way, you can place the seeds of different plants in one place, so you don't have to sort through lots of different containers. If, however, you are planting seeds to give or sell to others, it may be better to have individual containers.

Another good way of organizing seeds in one place is to use a binder with clear plastic storage pockets. The good thing about the binder system is that you can store different seeds in one place without taking up much room. When their pages are closed, the seeds will be in darkness, shutting air and moisture out.

One thing that beginner seed-savers often miss are the little details, like labeling and dating your seeds. Proper labeling is essential for organized seed storage. You should clearly mark each container, box or jar with the seed variety, date of collection, and any other relevant information. This helps you correctly keep track of your seeds' ages. Even stored seeds have dates that they should be used by, to maintain their quality. By properly tracking the dates of your seeds, for example, you will ensure that the oldest seeds are used first, whenever you are preparing your plants for the next season.

To catalog or label your seeds, you may find it easier to put the seeds in alphabetical order, whether in a binder or pill box. If you have separate containers to store each seed type, you can store them alphabetically with the A's on the top. You might also want to have a separate storage area for seeds from different seasons. For instance, you could use a separate shelf to put all of your Spring germinating seeds in. Use another for Summer seeds and yet another for winter seeds.

If there are seeds you use more often, you might consider storing these separately as well, to make it quicker and easier for you to access the seeds. For instance, seeds that can be planted all year round, would suit being placed on their own, in a place that is simple to access.

If you have a lot of seeds, you could download a seed organizer/tracker app. A good seed organizer app will remind you of things like how many days to leave your seeds out to dry, it will remind you of when to turn the seeds your drying out. It will also tell you when to plant your seeds, and how long it should take for different types of seeds to germinate. If you're busy, seed organizer/ tracking apps can take a lot of the guesswork out of what to do and when. Take the guesswork out of seed-saving by allowing technology to help you organize your seeds.

B. Creating the Best Storage Environment for Your Seed Bank

Now you have placed your seeds in an airtight container and properly labeled them. The next step is to place that container somewhere cool and dark. We've went over possible places early on in this book like refrigerators, freezers, etc. But we will add a few more places here as well.

A cupboard is a great choice as it's relatively small, is easy to open, and access your collection from. Other places to store your seed containers include desks and filing cabinets. Basements work well as they are naturally cool, being underground and less likely to be influenced by outside temperatures. If you must keep seeds above ground, you may need to use air conditioning in warmer months to ensure your seeds don't heat up.

Wherever you choose, be sure that your seeds remain in a dark place with a temperature below at least 40 degrees Fahrenheit.

Chapter 8

Book VIII. Germinating Saved Seeds to Grow Plants That Thrive!

A. Seed Scarification and Stratification: Enhancing Germination Rates

Seeds remain dormant in the wild in order to protect against unfavorable weather, pests, and environmental damage. Thickened seed coat or a waxy coating helps protect seeds and keep them dormant. However, nature has provided ways to overcome these barriers. For instance, freezing and thawing, being digested by animals and microorganisms all help to bring seeds out of dormancy.

Gardeners have had to find ways to break down the barriers to germination on their own. Scarification and stratification are two ways gardeners have found to help bring on germination.

Scarification

A seed's hard coat is broken down by scarification in order to let moisture in so the seed can germinate. Scarification involves cutting or scoring the seed coat with something sharp or abrasive, such as a knife or sandpaper. Sometimes shaking a seed or striking it is needed. For example, lightly tapping a seed with a hammer or another heavy object, or shaking the seed vigorously inside a container are examples of this method. Chemical scarification is sometimes used to break down the outside of seeds. Chemicals such as sulphuric acid can be used, though seeds should be watched closely. You do not want them to become dissolving to the point where they are damaged. An example of thermal scarification includes boiling water, and some skilled individuals have even had success using fire. Again, these methods take some care so as not to damage the seeds. Seeds that require scarification to germinate include sweet peas, beans, spinach, strawberries, and eggplant.

Stratification

Moisture, cold temperatures or warm temperatures are used to stratify seeds in order to bring on germination. In nature, seeds are exposed to stratification naturally during the cold, winter months. Springtime and warmer temperatures naturally bring these seeds to the point of germination. Gardeners can mimic this process by planting seeds out in the fall so they go through natural dormancy during the cold months. If you want to speed the process up, or if you live in a place that is relatively warm all year around, you can use refrigeration in place of true Winter in order to bring seeds out of dormancy. Wrapping seeds inside a dampened cloth and placing them inside a plastic bag before putting them into the freezer for 30-90 days, depending on the seed type, should suffice. Plants that require stratification include artichokes, sage, valerian, and rosemary.

B. The Ideal Conditions For Best Germination (optimal light exposure, temperature, moisture)

Seeds require optimal light, temperature, oxygen, and water to germinate. Perennials require chilling before breaking dormancy. When it's time to germinate, the seeds should gradually be exposed to warmer temperatures.

Other seeds only need warmth to germinate. Tomatoes, for example, require warm temperatures to sprout. Soils measuring 85 degrees Fahrenheit are best for tomatoes and peppers. Lettuce, on the other hand, thrives at soil temperatures of 60 degrees Fahrenheit. It pays to research the optimal soil temperatures required for every variety of seed you use.

Water is essential for germination to occur. Water softens the seed coat, swelling it and allowing it to split. Placing seeds directly in moist soil is sufficient for spurring many plants into germination. Other seeds, with thicker coats, need to be soaked overnight. Even others might need scarification or stratification instead of or in addition to soaking.

Seeds breathe, and their need for oxygen increases during germination. Well-drained, loose soil is the best for seeds to get adequate access to oxygen. Tight-packed soil may suffocate sprouting seeds.

Most seeds germinate in the dark and are best planted. A few require light to germinate. Plant these on top of the soil surface.

After germination, light is what seeds need the most. However, some seeds do better in full sunlight. You should gradually move these seeds from the shade into the light to acclimate them to more concentrated sunlight. Some do better in more shady conditions.

C. How to Prepare Soil For the Healthiest Seedlings

<u>Loosen Soil</u>

Using a gardening fork, dig the soil to loosen it, removing any weeds and unwanted roots. Continue to move the soil about until it's easy to get the fork through. This action will aerate the soil, allowing oxygen in so the seeds can breathe. Loosening soil also makes it softer so that the seeds' roots can grow more comfortably.

<u>Add Compost</u>

Seedlings are hungry. They need a lot of nutrients to grow. Before planting, mix high-quality compost throughout the soil to give the seedlings the best chance of reaching their potential. Rake through your seedbed to make it smooth, removing any weeds, stones, and other objects that may get in the way of your seedlings. The smaller the seed, the flatter your soil bed will need to be.

<u>Add Moisture:</u>

If the soil is dry, water it with small, widely dispersed drops of water so as not to create clumping. You want moist soil, not dust. Too much water will create muddy, thick soil that will damage seed roots.

D. Germination Techniques for Different Seed Types

<u>Stratification</u>

Plants that require cold to germinate must be exposed to cold temperatures, followed by exposure to warmer temperatures to bring them out of dormancy. You can plant them during Winter so they naturally come to life in the Spring. Alternatively, you may wish to store your seeds in the freezer until early Spring, and plant them at that time. Plants requiring cold treatment include:

Chives, ginseng, cilantro, echinacea, goji, hops, lavender, lemon balm, heather, goldenseal, licorice, mulberries, elderberry, thyme, valerian, witch hazel, vervain, cilantro, wild ginger, and catmint.

<u>Scarification</u>

Scarification involves cutting, piercing, nicking, crushing, banging, shaking, and other methods of softening the seed in order for the sprout to come through.

Plants that will germinate after scarification:

Lupine, milkweed, Joe Pye weed, morning glories, nasturtium, sweet peas, poppy mallow, columbine, moonflower, winter squash, bean and spinach.

Direct Planting

Plants that germinate quickly, without needing stratification or scarification, can be planted directly into the soil. In general, smaller seeds need to be planted at less depth than larger ones, but do your research on the seed variety to ascertain the required planting depth.

Grow Sprouts

In order to increase the number of seeds that germinate, you can sprout them before planting. Sprouting can be done by placing seeds in water between two pieces of paper and covering them with a liberal amount of water. Once sprouted, the seeds can be planted.

Germinating Seeds in a Paper Towel

One method that some home gardeners use to effectively increase the number of seeds that germinate, is to sprout your seeds before planting. Germinating seeds in a paper towel is a straightforward and effective method to initiate plant growth. Follow the instructions below to get started.

Materials You Will Need:

- High-quality seeds

- Unbleached paper towels

- Shallow tray or plate

- Distilled or filtered water

- Plastic zip-top bag or plastic wrap

- Marker or label for seed identification

Germination Process Follow these steps to germinate seeds in a paper towel:

1. Moisten a paper towel without soaking it.

2. Arrange seeds on one half of the paper towel, leav-

ing space between them.

3. Fold the other side of the paper towel over the seeds, then press lightly.

4. Enclose the paper towel in a plastic bag or cover it with plastic wrap.

5. Label and place the tray in a warm, well-lit area.

Monitoring and Care Ensure successful germination with these tips:

1. Check and maintain moisture levels in the paper towel.

2. Monitor seed progress for signs of sprouting.

3. Transfer the sprouted seeds, with care, into a suitable growing medium.

Germinating seeds in a paper towel is a simple yet effective way of kick-starting your plant's growth. By following these steps and carefully monitoring the progress, you'll soon witness the miracle of seed germination.

Hydroponic Germination

Hydroponic germination is a fascinating method that allows plants to sprout and grow without soil. Some gardeners enjoy germinating their seeds this way because you can better control their environment, you can increase your plants growth rate and get higher yields, you can grow plants in a smaller place, you can use less water, you have precise control over nutrient levels, and you reduce the risk of soil-borne diseases and pests in your plants.

If this method interests you, here is a brief explanation of it and how you can get started. Hydroponic germination is especially useful when outdoor conditions are harsh or the weather is unpredictable. If you live in colder climates, or climates where much of the year is cold like Canada, for instance, this may be a method you consider. Hydroponics is also useful if you're trying to germinate a plant that is difficult to sprout. Once the plant is robust enough to transfer, you can plant them wherever you choose during the seedling stage.

<u>Materials You Will Need:</u>

Seeds: Select high-quality seeds suitable for hydroponic cultivation.

Germination Medium: Opt for a suitable medium to support seed germination in the hydroponic system. Common options include rockwool cubes, vermiculite, perlite, or even a simple paper towel.

Container: Ensure it is clean and free of contaminants.

Nutrient Solution: Prepare a nutrient solution formulated explicitly for hydroponic systems. These solutions contain essential macronutrients, micronutrients, and minerals required for healthy seedling growth.

Water: Use clean, filtered water

Lighting: Provide adequate light for the germinating seeds. This can be natural sunlight or artificial lighting sources such as fluorescent, LED, or high-intensity discharge (HID) lights. Consider the light requirements of the specific plant species being germinated.

Temperature and Humidity Control: Maintain optimal temperature and humidity levels in the germination area. Use a thermometer and hygrometer to monitor and regulate these conditions, promoting successful seed germination.

pH Testing Kit: Regularly test the pH level of the nutrient solution to make sure that it falls within the appropriate range for hydroponic cultivation. Most plants prefer a slightly acidic pH range of 5.5 to 6.5.

Labels: For organizing the seed types and dates.

Protective Covering: Consider using a "humidity dome" or saran wrap to create a mini greenhouse effect and maintain a consistent environment for germination.

<u>Preparing Your Seeds For Hydroponic Germination</u>

1. Seed Preparation: Soak the seeds in water for a predetermined time, as specified for the particular plant species. This helps initiate the germination process.

2. Germination Medium: Choose a suitable medium for seed germination in the hydroponic system. Common options include rockwool cubes, vermiculite, or perlite. These materials provide support

to the seeds while allowing the roots to access water and nutrients.

3. Germination Process: Place the prepared seeds onto the chosen germination medium. Ensure that the medium remains consistently moist, providing a favorable environment for seed sprouting. Maintain optimal temperature and humidity levels for successful germination, typically between 70-85°F (21-29°C).

4. Nutrient Solution: Prepare a nutrient solution specifically formulated for hydroponic systems. Provide the necessary macronutrients, micronutrients, and minerals to support the initial growth of the germinated seeds. And follow the recommended dilution rates and nutrient schedules for the specific plant species.

Successful hydroponic germination requires careful monitoring and attention to detail.

1. Regular Inspection: Monitor the germinating seeds for signs of sprouting and root development. Ensure the medium remains consistently moist, but

avoid oversaturation that could lead to root rot.

2. Nutrient Management: Regularly check and adjust the nutrient solution to maintain optimal levels for healthy seedling growth. Avoid overfeeding or underfeeding the plants, as it can hinder their development.

3. Light and Temperature: Provide adequate light for the seedlings, using appropriate artificial lighting or natural sunlight. Maintain the ideal temperature range suitable for the specific plant species, promoting optimal growth and development.

Hydroponic germination opens up exciting possibilities for growing plants in a soil-free environment. By understanding the principles of hydroponics and following the appropriate techniques, you can successfully germinate and cultivate your seeds for planting!

E. Caring for Seedlings: Transplanting and Nurturing Young Plants

You've been nurturing your seedlings, and now it's time to plant them. But when do you plant your seedlings? Some plants are cool-weather plants, others are warm-weather plants. The cool weather plants can be planted in early Spring; the warm ones in Summer. Examples of cool-weather plants include brassicas (e.g broccoli), peas, onions, garlic, beets, and leafy greens. Examples of warm-weather plants include carrots, okra, summer beans, kale, collards, and beets.

In Spring, hardening your seedlings before planting is a good idea. This can be achieved by storing your plants in a shady spot and placing them in a sunny place for an hour or so at a time. Place them back in the shade immediately if they show signs of wilting. Slowly increase the amount of time you place seedings in the sun.

Before transplanting, make sure your seedlings are at least 2 inches high. It's best to plant them when there are at least 2 sets of leaves or four leaves in total. If the temperature isn't too cool - over 60 degrees Fahrenheit should suffice - it is time to plant your seeds. It is ideal to plant your seeds during or after it rains, that way your seedlings have access to plenty of moisture. If the weather is dry, water the soil before planting.

How to Transplant Seedlings

Use a dibber, a wooden tool with a rounded end, to make a hole in the soil. Alternatively, you can use a stick. Make sure to create enough room for the plant's roots. Dig a hole large enough for half of the plant and its entire root system to be under the soil. Do not squish the roots down. They need to have enough room to spread out. Try to retain as much of the soil that your seedling is in. Next, place your seedling into the hole you've made. Then, cover your plant so it's submerged in the soil to the halfway point. Press down the soil gently so that it holds the plant in place. Finally, water it liberally.

Tips and Tricks When Growing Seedlings

- Avoid giving supplementary food until at least 4 sets of leaves are out. Feeding too early may burn roots and new foliage.

- Look out for signs of damping off, which includes wilting plants and whitening on the soil surface. This is a fungal disease that can cause seedlings to wither and die. When growing your seeds, be sure to always use sterile soil to avoid passing on diseases. To treat, scrape off any white deposits on your soil. Place in sunlight to dry, and water from the bottom.

- If you've planted a lot of seeds, make sure to thin out plants to avoid overcrowding. However, wait until the plants are established so that you have extra in case of high mortality.

- Once you've acclimated plants to sunlight, give them as much light as possible. If plants are in the shade and aren't growing as expected, consider re-planting them in a sunnier area.

- Water every few days to keep the soil moist but not sodden to avoid overwatering, which contributes to disease.

- After a few days, give your seedlings fertilizer to spur growth.

- Treat leggy plants - plants that grow too tall and thin too quickly, by lightly brushing and fanning your plants. This will make them grow thicker stalks.

Chapter 9

Book IX. Overcoming Common Seed-Saving Issues

A. Dealing with Cross-Pollination and Unwanted Variations

Cross-pollination can add unwanted genetic contamination from outside plants. This is a problem, especially in heirloom varieties where genetic purity is so important. There are many things you can do to avoid cross-pollination.

- Place varieties that can cross-pollinate as far away as possible from each other. The further away plants are from each other, the less likely they are to cross-pollinate. There is still a chance of some cross-pollination by insects, for example.

- To avoid cross-pollination, it's best to plant wind and insect-pollinated plants at least 100 yards apart. These plants include radishes, turnips, cabbage, melons, beets, squash, broccoli, radishes, beets and carrots.

- It's less likely for self-pollinators to cross-pollinate, but it can happen. When planting self-pollinators, you can help prevent cross-pollination by planting flowering plants between different types of seeds. Self-pollinators include eggplants, lettuce, tomatoes, peas, beans and peppers.

- A further protection against cross-pollination is to bag the female plants in order to stop unwanted pollination. Bagging involves pollinating the female plant by hand and then placing a bag over it to prevent outside pollination.

B. How to Deal With Seed-Borne Diseases and Pests

Diseases

Viruses, bacteria and fungi can be carried on seeds. Bacteria on seeds is easy to treat, but fungal infections, less so. Viruses, in contrast, are easier to treat. Bacteria are susceptible to heat and, when inside seeds, are easily treated this way. Fungi, being hard-walled, are hard to kill organically.

- Seeds can be treated using chlorine, aerated steam, or hot and dry air.

- Natural Fungicides are successful in treating fungi.

- Some include dissolving aspirin in water and spraying it on the affected areas of your plants.

- Another example is to use apple cider vinegar, which you can dilute with water and spray on the areas you wish to treat.

- Fermentation of seeds like those of tomatoes is useful in creating good bacteria that can fight off bad bacterial infections.

It is important to treat all kinds of seed-borne diseases the moment you see them occurring. If some diseases are given a chance to transfer from the seed to the field, they are capable of destroying entire crops.

Pests

To prevent infestation of seeds by pests, you can set bait traps before planting to test the level of infestation. For instance, when using a grain trap, place around 10 ounces of sorghum seed in a hole, cover the hole in soil and mark the spot with a stick or stake. Repeat this every ten acres. Two weeks later check for wireworms. If there are more than two larvae, it can be helpful to treat the seed and soil with an insecticide.

Personally, we advise going for a natural insecticide over the traditional ones. Why? Because using natural insecticides or making your own is a great way to protect your plants without causing harm to beneficial insects, pets, or children. Some organic pest control methods include using neem oil, insecticidal soap, or homemade remedies like garlic or chili pepper sprays. These options are less harmful to the environment, yet are still effective at controlling pests. Before you get started, consider these tips:

- Avoid applying insecticides to plants that have recently been burned, and make sure they are adequately hydrated.

- Before spraying the plant, pluck off any diseased leaves one by one and discard them.

- The best times to spray are early in the morning before the sun hits or late at night when the sun has faded.

- Always wear gloves and a face mask when using insecticide, even gentle ones.

- Keep pets away from the area until it has dried completely.

- Test your solution on a few leaves before you apply it to the whole plant and observe for 48 hours for signs of burning or browning; if so, dilute your mixture and try again.

Here are some additional ways that you can prevent pests from destroying your precious plants.

Practice crop rotation: Crop rotation involves changing the location of plants within your garden every season. This technique helps break the life cycle of pests, which will reduce their populations over time.

Start seeds indoors: If you're concerned about pests damaging your seeds, you can start them indoors. By controlling the environment indoors, you can reduce the risk of infestation. Once the seedlings are stronger, transplant them to your backyard.

Use floating row covers: Floating row covers are lightweight fabric covers that can be placed directly over plants. They create a physical barrier that prevents pests from reaching the seeds or seedlings. The fabric allows sunlight, air, and water to reach the plants while keeping pests away.

Implement companion planting: Companion planting involves growing specific plants together to deter pests. For example, marigolds are known to repel certain pests. Research companion planting techniques to find combinations that work well for your crops.

Practice good garden hygiene: Keep your garden clean and tidy. Remove any fallen plant debris or weeds, as they can harbor pests. You will also want to continually inspect your plants for signs of infestation. If you see any affected areas, remove them to prevent the spread of pests.

Introduce beneficial insects: Encourage beneficial insects, such as ladybugs, lacewings, or predatory wasps, to your garden. These insects feed on pests and help keep their populations in check naturally. You can attract them by planting flowering plants or by purchasing and releasing them.

Learn about common pests and their habits: Educate yourself about the pests that commonly affect the plants you're growing. By understanding their life cycles and habits, you can take proactive measures to prevent infestations and spot early signs of trouble.

Keep in mind that preventing pest infestations requires ongoing effort and observation. You will need to regularly monitor your plants, stay vigilant, and take prompt action if you notice any signs of pests to prevent them from breeding, spreading, and causing significant damage to your crops.

C. Troubleshooting Germination Issues and Poor Seed Viability

Some seeds simply have a low germination rate. A solution to this would be to plant many seeds at once. It will prove helpful to do some research in order to find out whether or not your seeds have a high sprouting ratio.

For instance, here are some seeds that possess high sprouting ratios:

- Bean seeds (e.g., green beans, kidney beans): Beans are known for their high germination rates and are often recommended for beginner gardeners.

- Radish seeds: Radish seeds are quick to sprout and generally have high germination rates.

- Lettuce seeds: Lettuce seeds usually have good germination rates and can sprout relatively quickly.

- Cucumber seeds: Cucumbers are typically reliable in terms of sprouting, given proper growing conditions.

- Zucchini and squash seeds: These seeds generally have a good sprouting ratio and are relatively easy to grow.

- Seeds with Low Sprouting Ratios:

- Parsley seeds: Parsley seeds can be slow to germinate and may require some patience.

- Carrot seeds: Carrots can be a bit finicky to sprout, and their germination rates may vary.

- Onion seeds: Onion seeds can take longer to germinate compared to other plants and may require specific conditions.

- Spinach seeds: Spinach seeds can be a bit less reliable in terms of sprouting, and their germination rates may fluctuate.

- Pepper seeds: Pepper seeds can sometimes have lower germination rates, especially if the conditions aren't ideal.

It's important to note that the sprouting ratio can also vary between different varieties of the same plant. Additionally, proper seed storage, handling, and providing the appropriate growing conditions (moisture, temperature, sunlight) can significantly impact germination rates. This is why it is so important to properly harvest and store seeds. Always consult reliable gardening resources for the best practices regarding each type of seed you plan to sow.

Reasons Your Seeds Haven't Sprouted

If your seeds haven't sprouted when they should, they might just be taking longer to germinate. But several factors can also impact the rate in which your seeds sprout. Anything from temperature, soil condition, and moisture might not be quite ideal, causing seeds to sprout a little later. Try waiting a few days to see if they come in. As well, you may want to consider pre-sprouting your seeds in advance next time. Additionally, these factors can play a role as well:

- Your seeds may be too old, or they may have been wet just before storage. If unsure, do a germination test to find out if your seeds are still viable. If you find your seeds don't sprout, update with some new seeds. If you don't have any of your own, consider swapping seeds with people in your community.

- There might not be enough water. If the environment is dry, keep the soil moist. The trouble with most soils is that they usually rest on either the sandy side, with water draining away quickly, or the clay side, which is compact, making it hard for the water to be accessible to the plants. A great way to improve any type of soil is to introduce organic matter such as peat moss. Not only does this help absorb water and help disperse it over time, but it provides nutrients that the roots need. Adding these amendments not only helps your plants grow better, but also makes sure they can access the necessary hydration when the weather gets particularly hot.

- Many people understand that too little water can prevent seeds from growing and can kill them, but they are stunned to find that too much water in your soil can prove deadly for your seeds too. It can cause them to decay or drown! That is why, although water is essential for a seed's growth, it's important to keep the soil moist, but not saturated. You can usually tell that your soil is too wet if it feels sopping wet to the touch. If you are using soil that does not drain well, it may be beneficial to mix in sand or perlite to increase the drainage rate.

- If seedlings don't emerge in the amount of time it usually takes for that plant type to germinate, they may have been planted too deeply. If you do not see signs of germination, dig in a little bit. Your seeds may be struggling to reach the surface.

- Nutrient deficiency can show up on leaves. Pale yellow leaves suggest a nitrogen shortage. Deep purple under the leaves denotes a lack of phosphorus. Bronze edges suggest a lack of potassium. Try half-strength fertilizer to revitalize your plants.

Chapter 10

Book X. Expanding Beyond Your Garden

Participating in Seed Exchanges/Seed Saving Communities

Joining a local seed exchange group or starting your own is a great way to gain access to different types of seeds. You can also find many online groups, which can be a wealth of knowledge, resources, and support as you bond with gardeners worldwide. Keeping in contact with other gardeners is an excellent way to further your understanding of at-home gardening. And as you connect with gardeners from different parts of the world, you'll always have access to advice whenever you need it. In fact, having a large community of gardeners around you can allow you to participate in international global seed trading with people you know and trust. Some people trade or sell rare seeds that may only be available in their region of the world. Obtaining seeds from these individuals allows you access to seeds and food you may never have been able to obtain before.

Some organizations are devoted to exchanging seeds for free, and some require a membership fee to join. There are also many seed-saving organizations, such as *Seed Savers Diversity* in Canada and *Seed Savers Exchange* in the USA.

Once you've started to get the hang of seed saving, you can share your knowledge with others. Whether you want to create a neighborhood seed exchange group or you'd prefer to go wider by joining a national organization, becoming part of a group of like-minded individuals who value the importance of seed saving will bring you community, friendships, fun, and even more knowledge and experience from seasoned growers.

Chapter 11

Bonus Pro Tips to Take You From Beginner to Expert!

You can use a small fan to gently blow air over your drying seeds. This helps prevent mold growth and ensures even drying.

Try fermenting tomato seeds to remove the gel coating. Simply scoop out the tomato pulp with seeds, place in a jar, add water, and let it sit for a few days. Rinse and dry the seeds before storing.

1. Use a mesh laundry bag to hang and air-dry seed heads. It allows for good airflow and keeps seeds contained.

2. To separate seeds from chaff, try the winnowing method. Pour the seeds and chaff from a height into a bowl or container on a windy day. The wind will blow away the lighter chaff, leaving the heavier seeds behind.

3. Create your own seed tape by mixing seeds with a small amount of flour or cornstarch. Apply the mixture along a strip of biodegradable toilet paper or newspaper, then plant the strip directly in the soil.

4. Crush eggshells and sprinkle them around young seedlings to provide a calcium boost and help prevent blossom end rot.

5. Save and plant seeds from the healthiest and most robust plants in your garden. This promotes natural selection and helps develop stronger varieties over time.

6. Create your own seed packets using decorative paper or recycled envelopes. Label them with the seed variety, date, and any special instructions.

7. Save seeds from heirloom or open-pollinated varieties to maintain genetic diversity and preserve rare plant varieties.

8. Consider starting a seed exchange with fellow gardeners in your community. It's a great way to discover new varieties and share your favorite seeds.

9. To test seed viability, place a few seeds into a damp paper towel. Then, place them in a sealed plastic bag. Check after a few days to see how many have germinated. This gives you an idea of the germination rate before planting.

10. Store seeds in airtight containers, such as glass jars or resealable bags, and keep them in a cool, dark, and dry place. Consider adding silica gel packets to absorb any excess moisture.

11. Avoid storing seeds in the refrigerator door, as the temperature fluctuations when the door is opened can affect their longevity.

12. Use a desiccant like powdered milk or powdered clay to absorb moisture when storing seeds in hu-

mid climates.

13. Learn about your local seed laws and regulations to ensure compliance when sharing or selling seeds.

14. Keep a garden journal to record your seed-saving experiences, including details on plant performance, seed viability, and any observations or lessons learned.

15. Experiment with different germination methods, such as using vermiculite, coconut coir, or soilless seed-starting mixes, to find what works best for specific plant species.

16. Learn about the specific pollination requirements of different plants to prevent cross-pollination and maintain seed purity. Use isolation techniques or time your plantings strategically.

17. Engage in seed-saving communities and forums to connect with experienced seed savers, exchange knowledge, and learn about unique seed-saving techniques.

18. Consider using a seed-saving spreadsheet or database to organize and track your seed collection. Include information such as seed source, date saved, and any additional notes.

19. Explore the world of perennial vegetables and herbs, as they can provide a continuous source of seeds and food year after year.

20. Try seed-saving challenges, like attempting to save seeds from a new plant variety each year. It encourages experimentation and expands your seed collection.

21. Learn about seed-saving techniques from different cultures and regions. Traditional methods can offer valuable insights into preserving and propagating seeds.

22. Experiment with hand pollination to control cross-pollination and develop specific plant traits. Use a small brush or cotton swab to transfer pollen between flowers.

23. Understand the differences between dry-seeded and

wet-seeded plants. Dry-seeded plants have seeds that are easily separated from the plant, while wet-seeded plants require fermentation or extraction methods.

24. Practice seed-saving ethics by obtaining permission before collecting seeds from public or private gardens, parks, or natural areas.

25. Consider using organic and sustainable gardening practices when growing plants for seed-saving. This promotes healthier plants and ensures the integrity of the seeds you save.

26. Keep a backup supply of seeds in case of crop failures or unexpected challenges. It's always good to have a safety net for your garden.

27. Celebrate the diversity of seeds by exploring unique and lesser-known plant varieties. Step outside of the conventional choices and discover the wonders of heirloom, wild, and heritage seeds.

28. Always start with quality soil: Ensure your garden beds have well-draining, nutrient-rich soil. Add compost or organic matter to improve soil struc-

ture, fertility, and moisture retention.

29. Provide adequate sunlight for vegetables: Most vegetables require at least 6-8 hours of direct sunlight per day. Choose a location in your garden that gets ample sunlight, which will promote healthy plant growth and fruit production.

30. Practice proper watering: Water your vegetables deeply and consistently to keep the soil evenly moist. Avoid overwatering because this can lead to root rot, and underwatering, which can stress the plants. Instead, you may opt for using drip irrigation or soaker hoses, as they can directly deliver water to the plant roots.

31. Use mulch to conserve moisture: Mulch to conserve moisture: Apply a layer of organic mulch like wood chips or straw, around your vegetable plants. Mulching helps conserve soil moisture, suppress weeds, and regulate soil temperature.

32. Harvest at the right time: Harvest your vegetables when they are ripe and ready. Each vegetable has

specific signs of ripeness, such as color changes, firmness, or size. Regularly check your plants and harvest promptly to enjoy the best flavor and quality.

33. Water deeply and consistently: Melons and fruit plants require regular watering to establish healthy root systems and promote fruit development. Water deeply, allowing the soil to dry slightly between watering sessions. Avoid overhead watering to prevent foliar diseases and focus on providing water directly to the plant's root zone.

34. Use trellises or supports: Many melon varieties can benefit from vertical gardening techniques. Use trellises, stakes, or supports to train melon vines to grow vertically, saving space and promoting better air circulation. This also helps prevent fruit rot and makes harvesting easier.

By incorporating these bonus pro tips into your seed-saving journey, you'll deepen your knowledge, expand your collection, and become an expert in the art of preserving and propagating plant life. As well, by following these tips, you'll set yourself up for success in growing a bountiful and healthy vegetable garden. Remember to adapt your practices to the specific needs of each vegetable variety you grow. Enjoy the adventure and happy seed saving!

Chapter 12

Conclusion

The journey toward becoming a successful seed saver is one of getting started, trial and error, learning from your mistakes and trying again until eventually you figure out the methods that work best for you. It is not always easy. In fact, it can be lots of hard work at first, but it is fun and rewarding! And, it is a wonderful and practical skill that so many of us in the Western world have lost over the centuries as we've come to rely on groceries stores for our food.

Growing your own food is a way that you can take back your power, save money and be proud of the fact that you can be self-sufficient in a world where we are relying on major corporations more and more, to our own detriment.

At the end of the day, it is thrilling to regain the skill of being able to feed yourself and your family without a third party's assistance. And it is deeply satisfying to know exactly what you are eating, how your produce was grown, and which chemicals - or lack thereof - was used on your produce while it was grown.

As with anything worth having, there are obstacles along the way on your gardening journey, but discovering how to create a thriving garden is something so precious that no one can take away from you.

We made a promise to help you from the moment you harvest your first seeds, to cleaning, storing and planting your seeds for the next season. We've taught you how to make sure your seeds stay viable from harvest to storage to germination and beyond.

We know the journey toward complete self-sufficiency involves a lot of work, but as you can see, it's so worth it in the end. Now that you know how to grow your own seeds, go out and create your own perfect garden!

We encourage you to expand beyond your garden as well. You can always save seeds to swap, share or sell with others. You would be surprised to see all the seed-saving groups and organizations in your area alone. The past few years have awoken so many people to the importance of knowing how to fend for themselves. As well it dispelled the myth that grocery store produce is the best quality. It is not.

Oftentimes, that food has traveled so far that by the time it hits store shelves, much of the nutrients have degraded, and the food is already old! Growing your own food, and finding like-minded people to swap seeds, share knowledge and create community with is the way to go. It is the way of the future!

As a self-sufficient seed saver, you can feel secure knowing that not only are you eating the freshest, healthiest food, but you are saving money, and you will be prepared for whatever environmental, political, and financial obstacles life throws at you.

It is our hope that each day, as you look upon your wonderful garden, you take comfort in the fact that your quality of life and that of your family is dependent upon the miraculous little seeds gifted to us by nature. May you and yours always have fruitful and abundant harvests.